The Faulkner Tarot

*The first modern
Photographic tarot deck*

by
Rhiannon Faulkner

Published by Sakayi Publishing in 2009
Copyright Rhiannon Faulkner.

ISBN 978-09551902-4-7   Book
ISBN 978-09551902-3-0   Tarot Deck

The Faulkner Tarot

In Loving Memory of my darling husband Dave xxx

This deck has been created to try and make a difference in how people see tarot.

My one wish is to see all tarot readers, mediums and healers work in love and light, with the intention to help people through life's problems and show them a way to create their own destiny.

I should like to thank all the models who have given their permission to have their pictures used in the deck and a huge thank you to Natalie Rorie for taking the pictures.

10% of the profits from this tarot deck is going to Rhiannon's chosen charity each year, in the hope that we can make a small difference.

The Faulkner Tarot

How to use The Faulkner Tarot

Thank you for buying the first modern photographic tarot deck. You have taken the first step to help change the way people see and think of tarot.

This deck was created to show tarot as a modern form of self help or counselling. The frightening images have been changed and down to earth pictures of life's situations have been used instead.

Teaching tarot and giving professional private readings to people of all walks of life every day has shown me that this deck is essential to remove the idea that tarot is scary, evil and wrong.

The idea of talking to spirit, guides and deceased loved ones is frowned upon by so many people in this day and age and particularly using the tarot is seen as a way of dancing with the devil.

I want to change this way of thinking and bring tarot into the modern world. I believe in God, I have a very strong faith but for some reason I have been given the gift of clairvoyancy and the determination to prove that this does not make me a bad person.

When used in the correct manner, your tarot deck can help you find answers to all problems in your life and others. It can advise you of what is about to happen, what choices you will have to make and help you understand the underlying cause of reoccurring problems or the lessons you are here to learn in life.

Your tarot deck is just a tool that enables your guides to communicate with you if you cannot yet hear them or see them. After working with these cards for sometime, your intuition or inner voice or guides will take over and you will begin to hear, see or feel them.

When giving a reading, you are acting as a channel for spirit to speak to the person you are reading for. Learning the meanings of the cards in this deck is important for both you and your guide, making sure they know which card to give to you to prompt you in saying the right thing.

Take your time getting to know these cards, see it as a beginning of a journey. I have included many meanings for each card, never be afraid to use the book whilst doing a reading, to double check which key word is the relevant one this time. Don't be afraid to say the first thing that comes into your head - random thoughts that come to you are important and in time you will learn to trust that your guide is communicating with you in his own way.

When you first open the pack of cards, light a candle and cleanse them by holding them over the smoke of an incense stick. Take a moment to touch each card, studying the picture. This is putting your energy onto the deck. They are yours and yours only. They will only be touched by someone else when they have to shuffle before having a reading and then they are cleansed straight after you have finished.

The major arcana is the name given for the first 22 cards. These tell us a story of a cycle from beginning to end. Cycles in life that we have all been through, such as childhood and growing up and leaving home: becoming a parent ourselves and raising new souls:

When you first open the pack of cards...

1. There are 4 suits:

CUPS	Love	SWORDS	Troubles
WANDS	Work	PENTACLES	Money

These cards show us different stages in these areas of our lives. See them as rungs on a ladder, starting with the first step being an ACE and the top rung being a TEN.

Try and relate to each card and think of a situation that you have been through that the card would best describe. This helps in understanding what the person you are reading for is going through when that card comes up. You may not have been through the same experience, but you can understand how that card once felt for you.

2. The people cards in the tarot are very important. You need to acquaint yourself with your star signs and recognise the positive and negative sides of each star sign in order to be able to understand the person for whom you are reading. It inspires confidence, when the person for whom you are doing the reading feels you have a very deep understanding of their character.

Look at the picture in the card and study it carefully. Notice what part of the picture jumps out at you, as this is spirit trying to catch your attention. You may see the same card in many readings but notice different aspects of the picture each time.
Say what you see !

Remember to think positively with every reading. Even the worst experience that you have been through in your life got better eventually and life carried on. So always stay positive and look on the bright side - we are passing on good advice not doom and gloom.

Practise as often as you can whilst learning with this deck. Randomly pick two cards and see what story you can come up with, say the first thing that comes into your head, I find this is the quickest way of learning the meanings. Spirit will always make you remember the relevant meaning at the right time.

Give 100% to every reading you do for other people, know that they have come to you for advice, never abuse this trust. Don't let your ego get the better of you whilst giving a reading and remember that you are just a channel - it is not you doing the reading but your guides.

I feel it is important that all tarot readers help people see that the children of this world are so important as they are the future generation. They need to be helped and looked after. This is why it is so important to me that people understand the traits of these different star signs, making sure that children are not misunderstood or branded before they have grown up and the damage is done. All children are born as a blank page in a book and parents write the pages. Take extra care in explaining to parents how best their different signed children will respond, with love affection and patience.

Love and light

Rhiannon Faulkner

0   The Fool

Key Words: *New Beginning*

This is the first card of the whole deck. It symbolises a new beginning, a fresh start. This can be related to work, relationships or a particular chapter in the persons life.

What jumps out of the card at you?

Is it the rainbow in the sky - suggesting a happy ending, a good move.
Is it the water - if so, does it look murky or clear and refreshing.
Is it the woods - suggesting density, darkness and nervousness.
Is it the dark island - stranded, alone, isolated, or dry land and safe.

Think of a time in your life when this card would have appeared in your reading. Write of a time when you had a fresh new start, was it scary, or exciting?

1   The Magician

Key Words: *New Opportunity, Intuition, Gut Feeling*

The magician is a golden opportunity that appears out of the blue. In this picture we can see a path, a boat and also a bridge to take us to the right place. We just have to follow our gut feeling as to which one to take. There is no negative side to this card, as the magician always delivers a wonderful chance to better our lives.

When this card appears in a reading, it is telling you to follow your gut feeling and go for it! It also signifies that a fantastic opportunity is coming, either in work or in the emotional life.

Think of a time when the magician appeared in your reading, when you had a golden opportunity or strong gut feeling to do something or go somewhere that turned out right.

2   The High Priestess

Key Words: Learning, Guidance, Spiritual

This card is all about the spiritual side of our lives. It says we have
something new to learn. This is a mysterious picture, not quite telling us
everything. Time is needed to let the whole situation evolve.
The high priestess is a very spiritual card, telling me that the person I am
reading for is aware of their spiritual journey in life, or will be soon.
More often than not, this card says you have something new to learn,
involving studies in a new subject or career.

Think of a time when the high priestess would have been in your reading,
representing a time when you learnt something new, or had to be patient
and wait for a new idea to begin.

3   The Empress

Key Words: Mother, Material benefits

This card is all about a time of fertility and abundance. This relates to
pregnancy, motherhood, but also in a work reading - a project being born
and creating material benefits.
It can signify a pregnancy or a child being born or a wonderful devoted
mother.
This is a good card to see when someone has set up their own business,
telling you that it will do well if nurtured like a child.

Think of a time when this card would have come up in your reading, how
did you feel and what was the situation. Also note down your childhood
experiences and how you would like a mother to be.

4   The Emperor

Key Words: *Father figure, Material success*

The emperor can represent a man in your life who you look up to and gives you good advice. It is a very strong dynamic card indicating success, goals being achieved and contracts being signed.

When it refers to an actual person in your life, it can be saying that he is a strong influence to you. A husband, a <u>father</u> or a professional advisor or even your boss of whom you think highly. In a business reading, it indicates <u>material success.</u>

Is it the man that you first notice in the picture? This would say that you are talking about an actual person.
Is it the road - perhaps saying that he is on the right road to success.
Is it the building, indicating contracts and material success.

Write down who your emperor is in life, your father, your husband, your boss. Try and say why you look up to them and what you admire.

5   The Hierophant

Key Words: *Highest Guide Card, Doing the right thing.*

The Hierophant is a very serious card for me. The picture shows quite simply a church, indicating help from above. So many of us want help from above when we are looking for the meaning of our lives or are searching for answers. It represents a teacher or a religious influence in your life, advising you. It says there is a situation in your life that needs your urgent attention and you must do everything in the right order.

It is making you aware of the right and wrong in your life. You can be assured when this card appears in your reading that help is on it's way, or you will make the right decision.

The Hierophant's presence in a reading can also turn the entire session into a very spiritual experience. Often, it says that spirit would like to give a message from above, so become aware of how you feel, and follow your intuition.

Write down your views on religion, where do you think your guidance comes from if you don't believe in God. Think of a time when this card would appear in your reading - when did you ask for help with a problem and where did you go?

6   The Lovers

Key Words: Choices, Relationships, Decisions

The picture shows a couple firmly holding hands with a long path ahead
of them. This card has two strong meanings.
Firstly we need to look at the cards around this one in the spread to see if
we are talking about a relationship or a big choice in life.
If it is regarding a relationship, it can indicate a passionate <u>affair</u> or
partnership. Look at the couples hands closely. Note the path ahead of
them, does it look uneven or long and uncomplicated?
If the cards around the lovers are pointing to another situation in life, then
this one is telling you that a <u>big decision </u>needs to be made. It isn't going
to be easy, as it is a time of <u>dilemma. </u>Maybe not a decision that the
person wants to make, but a necessary one.

When would this card have come up in your reading? Write down past
relationships that come to mind, and any tough decisions you have had to
make against your will.

7   The Chariot

Key Words: *Emotional struggle, Journey by road*

The Chariot shows us a two way road, fast moving traffic, but not too busy. This card indicates that we can be pulled in two different directions emotionally, not sure what to do for the best. An <u>emotional struggle</u>, either involving another person or on an inner level between ourselves. Determination is needed to overcome the difficulties in life.

The chariot is also a travel card, it tells us that a <u>journey by road</u> will be undertaken and it will be successful and enjoyable.

Perseverance is needed in life and success will always follow hard work.

Write down when you have fought an inner battle with your emotions and note when you have struggled to get on with another person, but succeeded in the end.

8   Strength

Key Words: Bravery, Fearless

Here the picture shows us a lioness. She is calm and relaxed yet we all know of what she is capable.

This card tells us that we need to be brave in the current situation in our life. Women are seen as being gentle creatures, but when we find ourselves in a difficult situation, such as our children or family being threatened, the fire inside us rages. We all have an inner strength that only shows when it is really needed.

This card says it is a time to <u>be brave,</u> <u>overcome our fears</u> and use our inner <u>strength.</u>

Remember - a woman is like a teabag - you only know how strong she is when she gets into hot water.

When have you had to use your inner strength? Did you amaze yourself at what you achieved?

9   The Hermit

Key Words: *Waiting, Loneliness, Soul Searching*

The card shows a woman in deep thought. She is taking time to reflect on things that have happened. She is alone and unhappy. The benefits of wisdom, maturity, age and memory all stem from the passage of time and cannot be gained at a young age.

The hermit stands for a time in our life when we stand back and look hard at the situations we want to change. The chance to evaluate situations is now.

This card quite often simply tells me that a person is feeling <u>lonely</u> and is looking for something more in their life such as a new partner or a more exciting path to take.

When have you felt like the hermit? Write down what made you want to change things. How did it feel to be lonely, even if you were actually surrounded by people.

10   The Wheel

Key Words: *Change, New run of luck*

Life is like a wheel that never stops turning. Good luck cannot last
forever and neither can bad luck.
This is a simple card telling us that a change is coming. It prepares us for
a change in circumstances and is often related to money.

It indicates a new beginning or chapter in life and is very karmic. If you
have done good to others then it will come back to you, if you have acted
badly towards others, then this has to come back round to you too.

Write down when the wheel has turned for you. When did a chapter in
life finish and another open immediately? Was it a good turn of the wheel
or not? Try and give examples of both.

11   Justice

Key Words: *Legal Matters, Fairness*

The scales pictured need to be evenly balanced. This can represent our emotions or a situation in life. We need to weigh up each side of a problem or two peoples side of a story.

The justice card nearly always means a dispute or legal problem to me in a reading. Not always as far as court, but it represents a time when truth and honesty are needed to deal with a problem properly.

The right person always wins with this card, but only when they have evaluated their side and have been completely honest to others and themselves.

This is a very karmic card - if you have done wrong to others, then just watch it come right back to you.

When would this card have appeared in your reading? Is there a time when a legal matter was in your life, or a time when you had a dispute with a friend or member of your family? Did the right person win? Also, think of a time when truth and honesty were needed in an argument or work matter.

12   The Hanged man

Key Words: Waiting, Sacrifice

In order to gain something, you quite often find yourself having to give something up first. A woman wanting to have children, sacrifices a lot of her own desires, career or freedom in order to have a family. This card represents time stopped still, while we decide what to do.

The time needed to reflect on an idea is important, to make sure we make the right decision in life.

This card says in a reading that patience is needed and they have to wait for an idea to evolve. If it came up in the past, I would say that they have made great sacrifices to get to where they are today.

Write down how you have sacrificed either your time or your dreams for an idea or for someone else. What does the clock resemble for you in your life?

13   Death

Key Words: New beginning, End of a way of life.

This card represents a very powerful <u>new start</u> in life. It is all about a new beginning. Out with the old, in with the new.

The picture shows us a dark scary room that we are in, with an entrance being shown to a brightly lit path or corridor, leading to a new room. This symbolises an end to what we are experiencing at the moment and a bright fresh start. This could relate to career, relationships or emotional problems.

I would expect to see this card in a reading of someone who was going through a terrible divorce. The awful wrangles we experience that really get us down and we cannot imagine life getting better. Then the death card is toward the <u>end</u> of the reading, showing us that a whole new way of living is there for the taking., kicking in after the divorce settlement.

This card signals an unpleasant time ahead, it seems to last for at least three months filled with uncertainty or unpleasantness, but with a definite <u>positive</u> change at the end.

When would the death card appear in your reading? What stressful time have you been through that was actually necessary to get you on the right path in life?

14   Temperance

Key Words: Relationships, Patience

This is a beautiful card - all about the <u>patience</u> and calmness we need to
have in relationships. It could be mother - daughter, brother - sister,
husband - wife, colleagues, friendships etc.

The picture in this card shows a large group of children. Which one
captures your attention? Is it the closeness of the two bigger girls, telling
you it is a lovely amicable, caring relationship you are talking about in
the reading. Or is it the thoughtful girl at the front? Does she look lonely
and left out - would this indicate that <u>attention</u> is needed in a particular
relationship for the person you are reading for?

Anger is depicted on the little girl's face on the left. What does this tell
you?

When this card comes up in a reading it means you need to pay extra
attention to your relationships. Are you pulling your weight and being an
equal member of a team? Look around at the other cards next to this one
to see which relationship or part of life is affected.

Why would this card come in your reading? Write down which
relationships in your life are needing attention at the moment.

15   Devil

Key Words: *Fear, Dread, Self destruction*

This is a difficult card. It is normally about you rather than another person in your life. Your fear or refusal to admit to a problem such as an eating disorder, alcoholism, drug addiction - all the ways you are damaging yourself.

It says there is a block. You are preventing something good happening in your life, by being the way you are.

It is the fear of failing in a lot of cases.

In some readings this card represents a manipulative person or selfish person in your life. They are controlling you, maybe a controlling father or boyfriend or even boss making your life a misery. However, it is still your choice to let them be like this to you and the decision to let them go out of your life has to be made by you.

A woman in an abusive relationship has to become strong enough and have self worth before she has the strength to leave.

Where is the devil in your life? What do you do to abuse your body? Smoking, drinking, eating too much or too little? What are you scared of, what situation do you need to confront that would have a huge positive impact on your own life?

16   The Tower

Key Words: *Difficult times, Material Loss*

This is not a card to be scared of in your reading. It isn't a pleasant time
but it is necessary.
The picture shows us a contained fire. This tells us it is safe, nothing will
happen to us physically, but we have lost valuable items in the fire. Items,
that maybe we think we cannot live without.
This card indicates that <u>disaster</u> is going to hit our lives where <u>material</u>
possessions are concerned, such as losing your income, marriage
breakdown leading to losing your matrimonial home etc. But this card
always comes when it is necessary. Calmer times always follow and the
change was necessary.
It is as if spirit world gives you many chances to make the changes you
should but when the time comes and you haven't done anything about it -
they step in and fate takes a hand. Such as your husband telling you he is
leaving out of the blue, yet when you look back over the years, you
realise things haven't been happy and you should have seen it coming.
Or, you lose your job suddenly ,but years later you realise the new job is
ten times better than the old one ever was.

When has the tower hit your life? Looking back, can you see why it was
actually a good thing to happen? What good came out of the tower
experience?

17   The Star

Key Words: *Wishes, Hope, Good Luck*

This is the card of <u>recovery.</u> After the trauma of the tower card, this one brings a tiny ray of hope. It tells us that there is light at the end of the tunnel.

When this card appears in a reading, it says that <u>positive changes </u>are on their way, things are really looking up in the current situation.

The picture shows us a wishing well. This indicates that your dreams are going to come true. You can have what you want - think <u>positive</u> and aim for your goals in life.

Intention is what you have to have now. Be positive about what you want to happen and it will. There is a lot of <u>good luck </u>and magic around this card. <u>Miracles</u> do happen.

When would this card have appeared in your reading? What dreams of yours have come true or what situation had a miraculous happy ending after a long struggle?

18   The Moon

Key Words: *Caution, Problems*

This is the card of <u>caution.</u> It tells us that we cannot see a situation clearly. Things are clouded and we need to be careful before committing to something.

Time is needed to let a situation evolve completely. We need to be on our guard.

This card can also relate to health problems. Look around at the other cards next to it in the entire reading. If there are other health cards nearby, then this one is telling you there is a problem but the end result is not yet clear. Again, time is needed.

When would the moon card have been in your reading? What experience have you had where you had to be cautious before going ahead with plans?

19   The Sun

Key Words: Happiness, Success, Prosperity

There is not a negative side to this card. It means <u>happiness</u> in any situation that you are looking for in a reading. Moving house, then it tells you that you will find a new home, Wanting love, it promises you that you will find true love, Wanting children, they are on their way! Basically any situation is going to improve greatly for you.

The sun is shining down on you and happiness is nearly here.

When did the sun shine for you ? What situations in life can you think of that were truly happy times for you?

20   Judgement

Key Words: Change, Clean slate, Karma

The judgement card is a very karmic card. If you have treated others well then you too will experience the same. If you have behaved badly to others, then you can expect to be treated badly.

The picture shows us a new day dawning, your second chance is here. Take it, learn from all the mistakes you have made in the past. Look back carefully and decide how you are going to make this day different for the better.

This card gives a new start in all areas of our life - career, relationships, finances.

A fresh start , a better start or a huge change in your life style is here with this card in your reading.

When did this card come in your reading? Give examples of both good and bad karmic effects. Did you mess up a relationship, only to have that person walk out on you? Did you change a career path and never look back ?

21   The World

Key Words: Completion, Success, Karma Repaid

We have made it to the end of a cycle in life successfully! The world represents completion, a happy ending. We have achieved so much and learnt valuable lessons along the way.

Typical cycles that we will all experience are childhood, leaving home and maturing, becoming a parent yourself, watching your children leave home and becoming a grandparent.

In a reading, this card will signify a time of peace, happiness and contentment.

What cycles can you think of that you completed successfully? How about leaving school, how good did that feel ?

The Cups Family - Water Signs
Common Traits: Emotional, Loving, Sensitive
Star Signs: Pisces, Scorpio, Cancer

Mum

Dad

Young child

Young adult

Get to know these star signs and try and notice similarities of friends or family that you know of the same signs. They are loving, gentle people, their life seems to be all about the emotions of a situation. They get hurt easily and hate upsetting anyone.

We need to get to know this "family" as people in our tarot deck, so when they appear in a reading you can genuinely understand what kind of a person you are reading for or talking about.

Think about what kind of marriage a king and queen of cups would have? Very emotional I would say, which sensitive parent would take control?

Page of Cups

Key Words: *Sensitive Gentle Children, Good News*

These water sign children are a pleasure to raise. They are gentle, emotional, genuine, sweet faced thoughtful, reflective children. You cannot poke harmless fun at one of these children. They would take it so seriously. Joking about the state of a young girls hair would devastate her and she would probably refuse to go out until she had re-washed it! Looks are very important and life seems to be serious a lot of the time. They get hurt easily and feel very wounded after an argument or disagreement with friends. This is the child that thinks their whole world has fallen apart when they fall out with someone at school.

They are serious children, and seem to give any task everything that they have. They try hard at school and are very caring towards other children, especially younger ones. They seem to need one best friend to feel safe rather than be part of a large group.

When this card is not actually talking about a child. It tells us that good news is here. It is the start of a very happy event, news of a baby or good news coming in general. Always take note of the cards directly next to this card in a layout so you can see if it is talking about a child or an event.

Write down the names of children 0-18 you know that are cups. Note their traits.

Knight of Cups

Key Words: The Lover, Romantic

This card can represent a man or a woman, aged between 18 - 30.
They are on the lookout for the perfect love, never settling down until they find perfection.
The men can sometimes be classed as a bit of a jack the lad - very good at wining and dining a woman. They will buy flowers, chocolates and give their all to be the romantic one.

The women are the same, always searching for their perfect partner. They need affection, attention and real love to keep them happy. They won't settle for less. I find the majority of female knight of cups look for husband or settling down material in every relationship they have, not being happy with one night stands or pointless relationships.

If this card isn't actually talking about a person, then it is indicating that an offer or proposal is coming your way. Not just in the relationship side of life, but maybe a helping hand in a tough situation or business matter. When this offer comes, you can be sure that it is a good one that you can trust.

Who do you know that would fit in this category? Have you ever dated one of these people? If you disagree with my interpretation, then write your own findings of their characters.

Queen of Cups

Key Words: Mother, Caring, Kind

This card represents a wonderful maternal lady. She is <u>kind</u>, <u>gentle</u>, sensitive and often a vulnerable person. She is also very intuitive and psychic.

She devotes her life to her children and would prefer to be at home raising them fulltime than away working. Of course, life today means that most <u>mothers</u> have to work to bring in an income, and they manage both roles very well. But their family life is always top priority.
She is loved by all her family and large circle of friends. Everyone seems to feel the need to look after and protect her. It amazes me that most of these queens have parents who still feel the need to be there for her just as they did when she was a child even when she is in her forties!

The queen of cups has often been hurt in the past, (while she was on the search for love as a knight) and she finds it hard to forget any pain she experienced. They find it hard to let go of past memories.

What is your interpretation of this queen? Write down common traits of two friends or family members that would fit this category.

King of Cups

Key Words: Sensitive, Emotional, Kind

This man is a gentle, kind, sensitive kind of guy. He listens to your problems, feels for you and understands the world of emotions. He will hide his real feelings and thoughts when you first meet him, to make sure you don't hurt him first!

He would make an excellent counsellor, giving good genuine advice to all people.

He can be slightly selfish it has to be said, although in his defence, when he realises he has hurt you, you will end up consoling him! He does need constant loving and reassurance in a relationship.

When he has finally met his true love, he makes an excellent partner. Still the romantic, he won't let you down on valentine's day. As a father, he is gentle, hands on, loving to get involved with the upbringing of his children. He is perfectly capable of cooking, cleaning and changing nappies!

What do you know of these Kings? Write down your ideas and note similarities you have seen between friends or family aged 30 upwards.

Ace of Cups

Key Words: *New Chapter in Emotional Life*

A beautiful rose, indicating the world of <u>romance.</u> The ace of cups signifies something new in an emotional sense. A wonderful <u>new chapter </u>is about to blossom.

It could indicate a new romance, meeting someone new to fall in love with, or if the person you are reading for is happily married or in a secure relationship, it tells us that something even better is coming to add to the relationship, such as a baby, a wedding or just a new spurt of love in a bad patch.

There is no negative side to this card, always promising positive and pleasurable experiences.
If someone was wondering if their marriage would last, if they would survive through the seven year itch they were experiencing, this card would say yes.
If someone asked if they would ever meet a true love in the future, then again this card is saying yes, it is on it's way.
Look around the card to see what the other cards are indicating. If it was directly next to a page card or birth card, then you know instantly it is a child on it's way.
When would this card have come up in your reading? What new chapter in your life would have been shown as the ace of cups?

2 Cups

Key Words: *Beginning of a relationship, Choices*

Here we see two people joining hands, beginning a happy journey together. This card is all about having made the <u>decision</u> to be with someone, be it in a business or personal <u>partnership</u>.

It is always exciting when we first get <u>together</u> with someone. We can see no wrong in them, and always say how much better they are than the last failed relationship. We have great plans and dreams for the relationship to work and end happily.

There is an exciting feel to this card, full of energy and surprises and love. It is the joining of two people at the start of a <u>long</u> and successful journey together.

Take note of the cards surrounding this one in a spread, to let you know if you are talking about a personal or business partnership.

Write down how it felt for you at this stage in your life. Could you see no wrong with your new partner? Can you remember the butterflies in your stomach?

3 Cups

Key Words: *Celebration, Party time*

We all love being in love. That feeling of excitement, the thought that you will spend the rest of your life with somebody, making plans for the future.

This card tells us that real <u>celebrations</u> are here, we are taking a further step in a relationship by getting engaged, married, or having a baby. A happy ending is guaranteed with this card.

Look closely at the picture. Is it the ring that jumps out to you, or is it the lines on the finger? The ring would tell me that it is a particular occasion to celebrate that the cards are indicating. The lines on the finger tell me, there will be a long happy future for this couple, or that they have come a long way already.

When would this card have come up in your reading? Try and describe what particular event you are reminded of.

4 Cups

Key Words: Discontentment, Boredom

Here is our happy couple looking rather unhappy. What's happened? After the excitement of falling in love, making plans together, the party is over. The couple settle into the normal boring routine of marriage. The reality of real life kicks in all too soon after the wedding day, or the birth of a child. Sleepless nights, arguments and plain <u>boredom</u> take over.

Our perfect partner, may not seem as perfect as we once thought.

This is a dangerous time in any relationship, we might start to look elsewhere and think that the grass is greener. Other women seem so glamorous and carefree when a man comes home to a tired new mother. And other men look so exciting when a man is working all the hours he can to pay a mortgage.

Has this card been in your reading? Write about the times when you were fed up with a relationship and how it felt to be discontent with what you have.

5 Cups

Key Words: Sadness, One sided love

This is a sad card. Our lady is about to walk away from a relationship. This means that there is someone about to be left feeling very <u>hurt and rejected</u>.

The 5 of cups tells us that this relationship has hit a rocky patch, with one person giving up. There is hope though, it can be salvaged if we are careful. The lady is not out of the door completely, she could change her mind and give it one more try.

All five's in the tarot are karmic cards. This means that if you have cheated, or messed up a relationship in the past it will come back to you one day. Make sure you read the cards close to this one in the spread to see if they will make the relationship work.

Write of your own experiences of being hurt in love and how it felt. Write how you dealt with rejection, did you beg for a second chance or did you let them walk away?
Also, think of a time when you left a relationship, did you give it plenty of chances or did you leave too early?

6 Cups

Key Words: Depression, Wanting to change

The six of cups shows us a picture of a woman <u>looking back </u>at happier times. Memories that seem so far away.
With this card, we need to understand that the person you are reading for is very low or depressed. Some sort of counselling would be advisable to help them make the necessary changes in their life.

We are now wanting to make a situation better, move on to happier times. This card can bring hope for the future because the person has actually acknowledged that something needs to change and is now in a position to do something about it.

When have you been in this position? Have you ever had counselling and did it help?
Write down your experiences of wanting to change and make a relationship work.

7 Cups

Key Words: *Confusion, Choices*

This is the card of <u>confusion</u>. Things don't look clear when this card comes up in a reading. It tells us we have <u>choices</u> to make now and it says that we are not sure of which way to turn.

However, this card always brings <u>positive</u> choices. It brings new friends, nice surprises and <u>happier times</u>, once we have made the decision.

You must understand how the person feels when this card comes up in a reading, as it is frustrating not knowing which way to turn in life. It may relate to choices in work, relationships or financial matters or even spiritual development. Reassurance is needed that everything will be fine once the decision has been made.

Look around the other cards close by in the reading to indicate what the decision is.

When would this card have appeared in your reading. Can you remember how it felt to be stuck at this stage?

8 Cups

Key Words: *Walking away, Miserable times*

This card shows us a picture of a man <u>giving up</u> and walking away. He has packed up and made the decision to move on in life.

Sometimes, a situation or relationship is worth fighting for, but sometimes we know it would be pointless to keep trying.

Look carefully at the picture and decide if you should advise them to give things another go, or whether they are doing the right thing.

Be aware of how sad this card is, there is no feeling of contentment with making this decision at all, so we all need to be sympathetic to the person we are reading for.

When have you given up on a project or relationship. How did you feel, was it hard to actually pack up and leave? How long did you try and make things work before you finally left.

9 Cups

Key Words: ***Celebrations, Wishes coming true***

Here is a dream come true, this picture shows us a new born baby, perfect and everything you wished for.

The feeling with this card is overpowering. When this card comes up in a reading it says that you will feel over the moon, delighted and very lucky with the situation you find yourself in.

It is such a happy time, feeling really satisfied with where you are in a relationship or stage of life, you can assure the person you are reading for that things will turn out okay and to carry on with their plans.

This card is the wish card of the four suits - make a wish and it will come true when this comes out in your reading.

When did you get this card in your reading? What have you wished for that came true? How did it feel? Write down examples of dreams coming true, whether it relates to a job, finances, relationships etc.

10 Cups

Key Words: *Happy marriage, Happy ending*

This is the highest run on the cups ladder in the tarot. We have made it! This card is a happy ending to the emotional journey we have been through with this tarot suit.

Look back and see how your journey has been, high's and low's, but here with this card we are now celebrating.

This card tells us of marriage - a good solid marriage that will last. It tells us of satisfaction emotionally, you have achieved your dreams of having a family, gaining a home, and living comfortably and achieving your goals in life.

Complete and utter contentment with what you have is how you feel when you reach this card.

What situation in your life would have been shown as the ten of cups? Marriage, having a baby? What good news changed your life for the better?

The Wands Family - Fire Signs
Common Traits: Artistic, Hard Working, Determined
Star Signs: Aries, Sagittarius, Leo

Mum

Dad

Young Child

Young Adult

Get to know these star signs and try and notice similarities of friends or family that you know of the same signs. They are hard working, sincere, chatty and entertaining people . They are 'do-ers'- never afraid of hard work and like to be hands on. We need to get to know this "family" as people in our tarot deck, so when they appear in a reading you can genuinely understand what kind of a person you are reading for or talking about.

Think about what kind of marriage a king and queen of wands would have? Very fiery I would say, fighting to be top dog of the household.

Page of Wands

Key Words: *Active, Adventurous Child, New Idea*

The page of wands is an energetic child, always looking for more in life. They are active, often sporty and adventurous. They love to be outside and busy.

These children are the ones who will ask the question "Why?" to everything. They are constantly learning, searching for the true meaning in life. This quest continues into adulthood. They are eager to learn, do well at school but you cannot make them learn something they have no interest in ! You have to find a way of making them think that they came up with the idea themselves, rather than you telling them what they should do. Stubborn? Yes, but in a lovely way. They are wonderful children, who with good parents backing them, can achieve anything in life.

They fight for truth, never lie to one of these children. They need to be treated as mini adults at all times. Grant them some respect and you will have a good bond for life.

When this card is not talking about a child, it means a new idea or birth of a work or study project. It is a burst of a new energy that will lead to a successful job or business. It is only the start and there is a lot of hard work to be done, but you can be sure you are on the right path in life.

What fire sign children do you know, from the age of 0 - 18. Note their traits.

Knight of Wands

Key Words: Fun Loving, Outgoing, Social

The Knight of wands is a party animal. They could drink most other knights under the table, or at least will have a damn good try! They are fun to be with and very entertaining. This is the guy at the bar who would spend his last penny buying a round for his friends and telling very funny jokes to all who will listen.

They are intelligent people, and not afraid of hard work. They are hands on workers, often learning a trade that will see them through life. Many of them will want to be self employed one day, not enjoying having to do as they are told by a boss. They always seem to know instinctively a better way of working themselves and have high hopes of achieving their dreams. Most of them succeed very well.

They are loyal friends to have for any other star sign, However they exhaust most people with their non stop approach to life.

If this card is not talking about an actual person, it becomes a very good business card to have in a reading It signifies someone coming in to help or an amazing opportunity to make a business or career successful. It could also signify a trip abroad either to do with work or pleasure.

What knight of wands do you know? If you disagree with my interpretation, then write your own findings of their characters.

Queen of Wands

Key Words: *Busy, Independent Woman*

This woman never stops. We can see a picture of a lady working at home, laptop on the kitchen table, on the phone and assisting her children with their homework.

She is always busy, but with a smile on her face. She needs to be occupied and needed, wanting to help everybody she meets. This is the woman who despite having enough on her plate, would drop everything to help a friend in need.

She is a fiercely protective mother, and slightly too independent for any man. She makes a great friend, entertaining and loyal, with a large social circle. However, she could probably count her true friends on one hand, the ones that would drop everything for her at a moments notice in return.

As with all the kings and queens in the tarot, this card may well come up in your reading to indicate a time in your life when you will become more like her than your actual star sign queen. Starting a new job after having taken time off after the birth of a child and having to learn how to juggle work and home life for the first time. Or it could indicate that a woman with these traits is entering your life and will become a very good influence for you.

Which queen of wands do you know? Or when have you been more like this queen in your life?

King of Wands

Key Words: *Hard Worker, Dynamic*

The king of wands is a hard working individual. He sees himself as the provider in the family. He is a great father and husband, but isn't always the hands on kind of dad. His role is to bring the money in and provide the best for the family.

He is always working, and devotes a lot of time and energy to make a success of a business or career. He is good with his hands, has the gift of the gab and could sell snow to the Eskimos! He is a trustworthy man and usually loved by everyone.

He is a born leader in a workforce, giving encouragement to apprentices and wants to show them the way. He is a risk taker and a gambler when it comes to work and luckily for him, it usually pays off in his favour.

The fire sign trait of having passion for life can be seen in all the family members.. The king of wands is no different, he puts his heart and soul into providing the necessary money for his families needs. He doesn't earn for himself, giving his last penny to his wife to spend it wisely. He is a proud family man.

Which king of wands do you know? Note their traits.

Ace of Wands

Key Words: ***Inspiration, Spark of an idea***

The ace of wands is the birth of a new idea. The light bulb effect!

We have all experienced the <u>flash of an idea</u> out of nowhere, it's brilliant, we may not have all the facts yet, but we know the idea is right and going to work.

There is great enthusiasm when we are at this stage. We are full of energy and bright ideas. This could indicate the start of a new project or business idea.

This card signifies a fantastic opportunity coming our way, so make sure you say yes to an offer that comes out of the blue.

What does this card remind you of? Write down how you felt when you had an idea that you knew would work but you didn't quite have all the facts in front of you.

2 Wands

Key Words: *Decisions to make, Contract*

There is an anxious feeling with this card. We have to make a choice or a <u>decision</u> at this stage. Do we take the job? Do we sign on the dotted line? Do we set up that business?

We are gambling here, not sure of the outcome but prepared to take the risk. When it was just an idea with the Ace of wands, it was exciting, but now we are committing. It is nerve wracking, wondering if we are making the right decision.

If the person you are reading for is settled in a job, it could indicate a <u>new job </u>coming or a promotion. They still have to choose whether to take the jump or not.

Although it can be scary, there is always a promising future ahead. Look around the other cards to see if it is a wise choice or not.

When did you have to sign on the dotted line? How did you feel and was it the right choice?

3 Wands

Key Words: New beginning, Good news

We have made the decision in the 2 of wand stage. Now the first stage is completed - we have signed on the dotted line or <u>made the commitment </u>to follow through our new idea.

At this stage, we think that we know what the future holds and we feel pleased and excited. However, the reality is that the journey has only just begun. There are even more opportunities that come with this card. More scope for the future and more to learn.

This card also tells that another person will come along and assist us and be very helpful. It could be a work colleague, a friend or partner in business that will bring welcome help and support.

The hand shake in the card shows trust and faith in the other person, but it also tells us that we can't do it alone.

What stage in your own life does this card represent? How did the job or business lead onto better things that you did not realise would happen at first?

4 Wands

Key Words: Take a break, Holiday time

This card tells us to <u>rest</u> up and enjoy where we are at this moment in life. We have worked hard to get to this stage so slow down now.

You are achieving your goal and doing well. It is time to <u>relax</u> and maybe spend some quality time with your family, away from work.

This <u>holiday</u> or time off, is short lived however, it represents that terrible feeling of the last day by the pool abroad, knowing full well that work is piled up on the desk for you to return to !

When have you not listened to this card? Was there a time when you should have been resting instead of working all the hours God sent on a work project? Write notes of how you like to relax and switch off.

5 Wands

Key Words: *Delays, Problems*

Remember all fives are karmic cards in the deck. This is not one that we like to see in our readings as it tells us that problems are here.

This one says <u>conflict,</u> troubles, delays at work. It is a <u>stressful</u> time. It may be that a new person has joined the company and we feel that we have competition to contend with. Maybe your boss is on your back and causing you concern.

Or perhaps there is a shortage of work or orders for your company and it is a worrying time for all. The good side of this card is that it is only a short term problem and you will fully recover.

Lack of money or inspiration is also indicated by this card.

When have you experienced this card? Was there someone you did not get on with in a job. Has your business suffered hard times? How did the situation resolve itself?

6 Wands

Key Words: Success, Good news

This card tells us that we have something to celebrate at work. Good news at long last.

The picture shows us two men in the office really pleased about an order that has come through finally or having completed a job successfully.

If the person you are reading for is employed, then it could indicate a promotion or recognition for their hard work by the boss or company.

I find that this card also indicates a person's creative work going public in some way. Not the ten o'clock news necessarily, but maybe fame locally, a press release or people hearing of their personal victory locally.

When has this card come up in your reading? What have you achieved where people praised you and heard of your work or success? Have you had a promotion or recognition at work?

7 Wands

Key Words: *Testing times, Struggling*

The picture shows our man in a state of disbelief at work. Something has gone wrong or he has received bad news.

This card says <u>testing times</u> are ahead, problems or <u>obstacles</u> are in our way. Success is coming but a lot of hard work and a bit of rethinking is needed.

New challenges face you that you weren't prepared for and perseverance is needed.

Look at the other cards to see what this person is struggling with, is it another person or a situation . The message is to keep going and <u>learn</u> from this hiccup.

It can also indicate that you have to retrain or learn something new to be able to succeed. It could be telling us of something new to study to be able to put this problem right.

When has this card come up in your reading? What have you struggled or battled with and what was the outcome?

8 Wands

Key Words: Good news, Success

This is a great card to have in any reading. It tells us that good news is coming and <u>success</u> for whatever situation we are in.

The picture shows our man welcoming an associate. A business card exchanging hands, telling us that we have brought in a new face to work with. It could quite simply be telling us that new friends are coming into our lives that will make a pleasant change and it is a time of <u>hope and promise </u>for the future.

We have to discard old ways of working and thinking and make room for new ideas to unfold. Success is guaranteed with this card. It feels like we are turning a corner in our life.

What does this card remind you of ? Make notes of when people have entered your life and made a big impact.

9 Wands

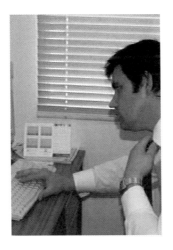

Key Words: *Crisis, Pressure*

Our man is feeling a bit hot under the collar now. The pressure is definitely on.

The calendar on the desk jumps out and tells us that there is a deadline, or time is of the essence. <u>Dedication</u> is needed now to succeed and not to give up.

We are in full flow of work commitments at this stage and can't cope with any more demands. The key to this card is do not give up, you will win the day but it is not going to be easy.

<u>Stressful times</u> is the easy way to remember this card, especially if it comes up in a relationship reading and has nothing to do with work. Deal with one problem at a time and give each one your full attention.

What time of your life does this card remind you of?

10 Wands

Key Words: *Burdened, Taken on too much*

The last run on the work ladder in the tarot and it is too much to take. We have given up and it is just too much.

Our man has thrown his paperwork in the air and <u>stress</u> has taken over. This card tells us that we have taken on far too much and can't cope. This card says we are <u>exhausted</u> and something has to give. Now we don't know what to do for the best to rectify the situation.

More often than not, this card is self inflicted. How many people do you know that make themselves ill with the amount of work they do, always offering to help others when really they can't cope with their own responsibilities. Family, job, second job to pay the bills…. We turn around and realise that we have actually expected too much of ourselves and now is the time that you need to accept offers of help.

A busy mother, with a day job, evening job and five children needs to accept help when it is offered occasionally instead of pretending to be super mum.

When have you been in this state? Stressed and unable to cope with your workload? Did it affect your health?

The Swords Family - Air Signs
Common Traits: Professional, Clever, Sharp
Star Signs: Gemini Libra Aquarius

Mum

Dad

Young Child

Young Adult

Get to know these star signs and try and notice similarities of friends or family that you know of the same signs. They are thinkers and very intelligent, clever, sharp people. They are professional business people.

We need to get to know this "family" as people in our tarot deck, so when they appear in a reading you can genuinely understand what kind of a person you are reading for or talking about.

Think about what kind of marriage a king and queen of swords would have? Very calm, rational but maybe a little too serious together?

Page of Swords

Key Words: *Intelligent, Boisterous children*

These children are often misunderstood. More often than not they seem uncontrollable, restless and impatient.

Truth is, they are <u>highly intelligent</u>. This is why they get bored easily. They need entertaining or educating the whole time. While other star sign children are taking their time to digest what they are being taught at school, this child has got it the first time they have been told. This maybe why they become restless and bored. They only need to be told once. So many times this child is classed as the naughty one at the back of the class, they are not naughty, they are bored.

The picture purposely shows us active energetic children burning off their excess energy. When this card comes up in a reading you must realise the potential of this child. The parent needs to be told how to deal with them. They cannot be left to sit quietly on the sofa whilst the mother cleans, they need to be involved and constantly learning and using their brain.

Often, spirit gives us this card, to indicate a child causing concern, regardless of what star sign they really are.
If this card is not talking about a child, then it indicates a <u>new idea</u> or concept. You need to have a rational mind and be open to the idea of <u>learning and developing new skills.</u>

Do you know a child like this? Note down your own interpretation of these children.

Knight of Swords

Key Words: *Strong, Assertive, Clever*

The knight of swords can be quite a ruthless person. It maybe upsetting to hear, but it depends completely on their childhood as to how they turn out as a young adult.

They are lively, assertive, strong and extremely clever. They are destined to be business people, high up in professional services. This is brilliant if they have been taught right from wrong in childhood, but what happens if they were classed as the naughty child at the back of the class who was misunderstood and thought of as trouble?
The man in the picture now looks shady, and devious. A mixture of being clever and troublesome could spell disaster.
Even with the loveliest of knight of swords that you could meet, they are busy energetic people who flit from one thing to another. Dynamic and determined, they strive to achieve their goals in life, leaving most other star signs far behind!

When this card is not referring to an actual person, it indicates that swift change is coming, often bringing chaos. Or it could indicate that a person is coming in who you need to look out for.

What knight of swords do you know? Give good and bad examples if possible. If you disagree with my interpretation, then make your own notes.

King of Swords

Key Words: ***Clever, Strong, Professional man***

Now our child has grown up to the age of 30 or over and has matured into a fine specimen. He is someone in authority, trustworthy and dependable.

Often in a 'suited and booted' profession, such as a doctor, solicitor, policeman, army etc, he is a very clever guy.

This man always seeks the truth in every situation, and finds a fair and just answer to all problems. He will not fight nastily, but seeks justice every time.

He is now the sort of man that we would all go to, to help us sort out a problem, knowing that he is genuine.

This card can also be linked to the legal profession or matters involving the law.

What king of swords do you know? Note their traits.

Queen of Swords

Key Words: Clever, Sharp, Intelligent

This queen is business minded , being very <u>logical</u> and knows exactly what she wants.

She has <u>high morals</u>, expecting the best of everybody, including herself and pushes herself to the limit. She can be <u>easily disappointed</u> by others yet she is charming and civilised to be with. She just has high standards. This makes her perfect for a management position.

The queen of swords beats herself up by analysing every situation, weighing up the pros and cons before making a decision. Actually this makes her a clever lady, thinking before she takes action, especially in business.

I find a lot of these ladies are divorced or single, as they would rather go without than stay with someone or something that is not perfect.

She comes across as a very fair mother, being protective yet fair, serious yet interesting at the same time.

What queen of swords do you know? Note their traits.

Ace of Swords

Key Words: *Challenge, Powerful new beginning*

The picture shows us a lady sky diving. This is a <u>scary</u> yet exciting venture for her to take. The ace of swords is like all aces, a <u>new beginning</u> in your life. This one is not always pleasant, or what we had planned. It feels like a <u>challenge</u>, we are never sure how it is going to turn out and we might fight against having to do it.

However, this ace always happens for the best. It is a <u>powerful new start</u> in our life that we look back on and say "Thank God I took the plunge".

A perfect example would be losing your job and being forced to try something new. Or your partner leaving you and having to start life as a single person suddenly. Years later, we look back and see that if we hadn't lost our job or marriage, we wouldn't be in the fantastic job or new relationship that we are in now.

Think carefully if this card came up to answer a question such as - Can I trust my new business partner? - Should I trust this new boyfriend? Suddenly, the thought of jumping out of a plane doesn't sound too good does it ? So remember , this card says we wouldn't choose this adventure if we had a choice. In some cases this card is a negative one. Always look around at the other cards to give you more detailed answers.
Give examples of when you have taken a scary new leap in life and write down the good / bad things that came of that decision.

2 Swords

Key Words: Decision time, Change

Here the picture shows us two paths. We now have to make a decision as to what we are going to do , or where we are going to go. Tense times are indicated by this card.

It could be an emotional problem, or a choice that we have to make regarding work or career.
Arguments, splits and upsetting times come with this card, but things will get better as soon as we have made a choice.

We all have a tendency to shy away from making a decision that we don't like, it is a lot easier if we just ignore the truth or problem. This card does not go away though, get it sorted at this stage and you will save yourself a lot more heartache.

When have you experienced tense times in having to make a decision. Write down how you felt and if you felt relieved after having made the choice.

3 Swords

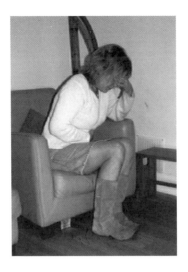

Key Words: *Heartbreak, Sorrow*

This card is not the nicest one we want to see in our reading. It indicates really hurtful and upsetting times. The lady in the picture is alone, and looks as if she could actually be in pain.

Heartbreak, illness, note how she seems to be cradling her stomach. Physical illness and health problems can be found with this card in a reading.

Hurtful and painful situations such as separations, arguments and really tense times can be traumatic to experience. However, we have to remember that no matter how bad a time we are having, we do always heal. Life goes on and eventually things have to get better.

What time in your life would you associate with this card? Have you had your heart broken, or lost something or someone?

4 Swords

Key Words: Rest, Slow down

Here our lady is sleeping. This card tells us to slow down and take time out to recuperate after a busy or stressful time.

This card says we need to take time out to think about our next move in life, relax and do not rush into making a decision yet.

It could also indicate that an idea will take longer than we planned to evolve, meaning that we will be forced to wait before we go ahead with our plans.

What time in your life were you forced to wait or rest up? After an operation or illness, or maybe certain plans such as moving house were delayed. How did it feel to you and did it all turn out for the best in the end?

5 Swords

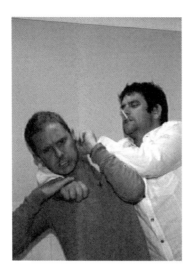

Key Words: Conflict, Arguments

This card is bad news in any reading I am afraid. It tells us of conflict and defeat either at work or in a relationship.

Violence can also be depicted by this card. Think very carefully before taking on a project or getting involved with someone if this card comes up, as it says it will not work.
This is almost like the 'NO' card - No to any question you ask the tarot to answer.

A task that you have undertaken will not go as planned and you will end up feeling humiliated or embarrassed.

It tells us of a struggle or battle ahead, arguments, tempers flying and failure.

When have you gone ahead with something when deep down you knew it wouldn't work? What wrong turning have you made in life that friends warned you of?

6 Swords

Key Words: *Positive change, Better times*

An end to a difficult period is nearly here. This card is all about sailing away from your problems. Here we have the same boat as shown in the magician card, indicating that an opportunity to change a situation is possible.

The six of swords says that we need to do anything possible to change the situation we are in, such as change job, move house, end a relationship. There is light at the end of the tunnel but we need to instigate the changes.

The boat shows us that the way out of the current problems is there, ready for us to take. When this card comes up you can be assured that things are going to be a lot calmer soon.

When would this card have come up in your reading? What difficult cycle have you experienced and what change did you enforce to make things better?

7 Swords

Key Words: Bad luck, Deceit

This card tells of a time of <u>bad luck </u>to do with the person you are reading for personally or a situation they are contemplating taking on.

Bad luck in choosing whom to trust, getting involved with the wrong person, <u>devious</u> people, or people <u>not being completely honest </u>with you.

When this card comes up, you need to be diplomatic and use tact when dealing with other people. Do not let them control you or rail road you into a decision. Remember that this card is telling you that you do not know all the facts.

Have you ever experienced this card? Have you gone into a situation not knowing all the facts and regretted it soon after? Have you been fooled by another person?

8 Swords

Key Words: Worries, Feeling trapped

The eight of swords is all about our <u>fears</u>. Here we can see a woman so scared that she is hiding behind a door. She seems petrified, hiding her face, not wanting to confront her fears. This card tells us that the person we are reading for is <u>feeling trapped</u> in a situation, not sure of which way to turn for the best.

However, usually this card tells us of our <u>worries</u> rather than real threats. It indicates that we are frightened of making a decision, and thinking of possible problems that haven't actually happened yet. It says we have to <u>make a decision</u> now.

The phrase, damned if you do, damned if you don't relates to this card very well.

When would this card have been in your reading? Was there a time when you worried about something unnecessarily. Were you too frightened to make a decision and how did it feel when you finally made your mind up?

9 Swords

Key Words: Sad ending, Sorrow

The nine of swords represents a <u>sad time</u> in life. It shows a situation such as a marriage, relationship, job or plans of any sort coming to an <u>end.</u>

This is not one we want to see in our readings, but it is often necessary. All things have to come to an end, especially if they are not right for us in the first place. Remember that life does go on and you will eventually get over even the worst experiences.

The <u>fear</u> that comes with this card is often worse than the actual ending of a part of our life. The worry that we put ourselves through when we can see that a relationship is not working, or if we know that we could be made redundant is petrifying. We are all capable of making ourselves ill through worrying.

Look around the other cards carefully to be sure of what part of their life is coming to an end.

When would this card have appeared in your own reading? What ending have you experienced and did you get over it ?

10 Swords

Key Words: A Final Ending, Loss

The picture shows something having been bulldozed and demolished. This card tells us that a part of our life has come to an <u>end</u>. It is a sad time coming to terms with our <u>loss</u>, be it our job, marriage or dreams flattened.

This card does not come out of the blue, there is always a build up to the <u>devastation</u>. For example, if this card indicated an ending to a marriage, then the marriage would have been on the rocks for some time, if it indicated a job loss, then this would have already been on the mind of your client. If the card was talking about financial ruin, then the debt problems would have been building up over time.

As hard as it is, no matter how much it feels like we have lost our entire world, we have to come to terms with this stage and realise that life still goes on. We can <u>rebuild</u>.

Look around at the entire theme to the reading to see what area of the client's life is coming to an end i.e. work or relationships.

When has this card come in your reading? What area of your life has come to a terrible end? What good came out of it ?

The Pentacles Family - Earth Signs
Common Traits: Materialistic, Good business
people, Like their creature comforts
Star Signs: Taurus, Virgo, Capricorn

Mum

Dad

Young Child

Young Adult

Get to know these star signs and try and notice similarities of friends or family that you know of the same signs. They are down to earth people and very hard workers, and enjoy the material side of life.

We need to get to know this "family" as people in our tarot deck, so when they appear in a reading you can genuinely understand what kind of a person you are reading for or talking about.

Think about what kind of marriage a king and queen of pentacles would have? Traditional standards, always aiming for the best and the high life?

Page of Pentacles

Key Words: Gifted, Quiet, Talented

The page of pentacles is an amazing child. Quiet, talented and very gifted. This is the child that belongs on the stage, whether it is acting, singing or dancing. They shine when they have an audience. This is the child who loves to dress up and will quite happily walk down the high street in a Minnie mouse outfit, loving all the looks she gets!
They take learning seriously and devote their time to studies. They are the quiet child in the class who is a pleasure to teach for any teacher, as they really enjoy learning and give it their best. They mix better with older children or adults, rather than children of their own age.
They already show the signs of liking a materialistic life - always taking great pride in how they dress. They are good at saving pocket money, quickly realising that if they want something in life, they need to save paper money for it !

These children need encouraging all the way. They need routine and cannot be rushed. This is the child who likes to know what they are doing the next day in advance, so they are not panicked. Simple things like laying their clothes out the night before helps and sticking to the same order of getting ready for school prevents any panic or fluster.
If this card is not talking about an actual child, then it is telling you of a start to a very successful chapter in your life, relating to money or material matters.

What page of pentacles do you know? Note their traits.

Knight Of Pentacles

Key Words: Hard worker, Materialistic

The knight of pentacles has now matured into a fine young adult. They are aiming for the top, wanting to be successful, rich and quite possibly famous.

This man looks like a dreamer, destined to be <u>successful</u> in his chosen career. These people <u>work hard</u> and they know exactly where they are going. He takes great pride in his clothes, often only wearing designer items or labels and always scrubs up well !

They are not frightened of a long journey to the top. They will plod along quite happily through years of studying if that's what it takes, to get to the job they set their heart on. Many other star signs would have got fed up and detoured yet these guys stay on the right path.

Their dreams of becoming successful are so real for them, they never change course. They are nice <u>genuine, trustworthy</u> people, very <u>traditional</u> and still need love and security from their loved ones.

This knight reminds me of an actor in between jobs, waiting for the call from Hollywood. He could go one way or another, successful through hard work, or lazy, waiting for the right break to come to him - and not giving up on the waiting!

If this card does not relate to an actual person, then it is telling you of a <u>long journey</u> that, after much effort, will be <u>successful</u> financially.
What knight of pentacles do you know? Note their traits.

King Of Pentacles

Key Words: Business Man, Self made

This is now a <u>successful man</u>. His hard work and dedication over the years has paid off. And he is lovely with it!
He loves the finer things in life, money, possessions, good food and fine wine. He has earnt everything he owns.
The king of pentacles is <u>money orientated</u> and seems to have the <u>midas touch</u> - he is the jammy one that always gets to where he wants.

He is a <u>trustworthy</u> husband, a true gentleman to do business with and a wonderful father. Everything he earns is for his family, making sure they have the best that he can afford. He takes great pride in his possessions, always liking the fast cars and beautiful houses.
This card can also indicate a man of this description coming into your life to help you with <u>financial matters</u>, such as a boss, or financial advisor. Listen to what this person tells you as they are <u>genuine</u> and can help you with money matters.

If this card is not talking about an actual person, then it is telling us that a payout of some sort is coming. Not necessarily winnings, but a large amount of money such as a loan, a pay rise, basically <u>extra money</u> that you haven't had to earn.

What king of pentacles do you know? If you do not agree with my interpretation then write your own here.

Queen Of Pentacles

Key Words: Financially independent, Traditional

The queen of pentacles is a quiet <u>traditional</u> lady. She is just as <u>materialistic</u> as the king of pentacles and works just as hard. It is important to this woman to have her own money. Even if she doesn't work, she will usually have housekeeping money that she keeps separate from the joint account to spend on her choices.

This woman makes a fantastic <u>business woman</u>. Devoted to making good money, she would be great at running a business.

She has old fashioned views, and <u>traditional values</u>, this is the woman that would be prepared to stay in an unhappy marriage because it was the right thing to do for the children. She always puts other peoples feelings first before her own, and seems to be the go-between in disputes, trying to keep everyone happy. If her husband and children didn't get on, she would be the one explaining to each party what the other one really meant, trying to smooth over any problems.

This woman wouldn't drink cheap plonk, she would rather go without until she can afford a decent wine! Image matters to her and you will find her home is like a show house. She is very <u>generous</u> ,always giving money or gifts to others without a second thought. She is a genuine lady and a fantastic friend to any star sign.

What Queen of pentacles do you know? Note their traits.

Ace Of Pentacles

Key Words: ***Cash Gains, New Chapter Financially***

All aces are a new beginning or chapter in our lives. This one is telling us of a new beginning in a financial sense. There is no bad side to this card, as it indicates we are going to be gaining in a <u>materialistic</u> way.

A <u>better job</u>, a large <u>pay rise</u> or even a house move to a bigger or better house. A home that we will be delighted with - a step up on the property ladder.

This card tells that money is coming to us in some way. It indicates a time when we could afford a little luxury in our life. Remember, each person has their own opinion as to what luxury means, to one man it would be a Porsche, to another, it would just be being able to afford any car !

The ace of pentacles is an <u>excellent card</u> to have in any spread, telling us the start of a successful venture is here. We are on the <u>road to success</u>.

What time in your life would this card represent?

2 Pentacles

Key Words: *Money problems, Tense times*

Here is our man at a cash point, unable to get any funds. He
looks concerned, with his head in his hands.
With this card, comes <u>choices</u>. We have to make a decision
now. We are <u>juggling</u> money from left to right, robbing Peter to
pay Paul. It cannot continue. This is the start of a serious
financial problem, but it can be dealt with now, to prevent it
from becoming any more serious.

This is a <u>tense time</u> financially, and this card says <u>be careful</u> with
all financial matters.

When has this card come up in your reading? Did you get it
sorted promptly or did you ignore the situation?

3 Pentacles

Key Words: *Apprentice, Using your talents*

The three of pentacles, comes after a lot of <u>hard work</u>. It could indicate a <u>new job</u>, or a new trade. Our man is on the tools, using his <u>talents to earn money</u> at long last.

He is at the start of a promising career, on the bottom rung of the career ladder, but with his foot firmly on the right ladder.

The only way is up now, <u>learning</u> more on the way. This card brings more opportunities to further or better yourself.

In some cases, it refers to actual DIY or home improvements. Look around the cards to see if it is talking about a job or the home.

When would this card have appeared in your reading?

4 Pentacles

Key Words: Saving, Investing wisely

The four of pentacles indicates a time when we have to <u>be careful </u>with our money. Time to put it away, as we will need money to fall back on soon.

Look after the pennies and the pounds will look after themselves!

This card acts as a warning that you need to <u>stop spending </u>and hold on to the purse strings.

It can also indicate that it is time to <u>invest</u> into something,. Maybe a business or property.

When would this card have come up in your reading? Give examples of both meanings, having to save, and investing into an idea or item.

5 Pentacles

Key Words: ***Money worries, Financial problems***

This card is a not a good one to have in a reading. It tells us that there are serious financial problems here now. We obviously didn't listen at the two of pentacle stage, and we didn't put money away at the four of pentacle stage either.

Now we are hard up. This could mean enforced change, having to change direction or our plans, due to lack of money. But don't give up, keep going as hard as it may be.

This card brings sorrow, and hardships, it says an idea is not going to work now.

Look around at the other cards close to this one in a spread, to see what needs to change or what area of their life has to change.

When would this card have appeared in your reading?

6 Pentacles

Key Words: Money coming, Generosity

This card brings money. The right amount of money. It says that just enough to get you out of hot water is on it's way to you.

The exact amount of money is being counted out in the picture. This card has a magical side to it, as the helping hand can appear in many ways. A tax rebate, that is almost exactly the same amount as your overdraft, a £10 win on the lottery that pays for the much needed trainers for your toddler.

It can also work the other way too, indicating that you are having to spend out a lot on others - bailing out teenagers or friends, or simply a lot of bills needing paying at the same time all of a sudden.

What does this card remind you of? Have you had a mystery helping hand financially? Have you had to pay out for other people's needs?

7 Pentacles

Key Words: *Decisions, Financial worry*

This card shows a woman pausing to decide what to do with her money.

She has two piles, one big, one small. She has worked very hard to get to where she is now, but she has a big decision to make, whether to carry on or change direction with a new idea to earn money.

This card says it is slow growth money wise, but don't give up, it will be successful eventually.

There is a pause in progress with this card, while we evaluate our achievements. Tiredness and exhaustion come with this card, but the key is to keep going with whatever decision you make.

What does this card mean to you? Have you been fed up with a part of your life, did you eventually give up or did you stick with it?

8 Pentacles

Key Words: Promotion, Success

This card brings <u>good news</u>. Promotion, a <u>new job</u> or profession all thanks to our hard work and efforts.

It says that we have been <u>recognised</u> as talented, good at our job and people trust us .

A lot of effort is needed to continue to prove ourselves but <u>success</u> is guaranteed at the end.

Have you been promoted? How did it feel? Or have you started a new job that propelled you up the career ladder?

9 Pentacles

Key Words: ***Financially secure, Material benefits***

We are so nearly there with this card! Life is good, we are <u>secure</u> and happy with our position in life.
Our man in the picture looks relaxed, content and enjoying a glass of fine wine. He has come a long way and deserves a little of the high life.

The nine of pentacles says we have achieved so much and can pat ourselves on the back for all our hard work. We can now afford a little <u>luxury</u>!

This is the card of enj<u>oyment</u>, times are good and we are <u>happy</u> with what we have or where we are in life.

What time in your life would this card resemble? When have you been at your happiest or most successful financially?

10 Pentacles

Key Words: ***Success, Achievements***

The ten of pentacles shows us a picture of a nice family home.
Through our tarot journey we have learnt by now that being
successful in life isn't about money, but <u>family</u>.
<u>Home</u> is where the heart is. This card indicates that we have
achieved real <u>satisfaction</u>, contentment and <u>happiness</u> in our life.

These <u>changes</u>, whether they be a new addition to our family,
marriage, stability or income, are going to make a <u>permanent</u>
change for the better to our lives.

We often leave our family home to our children in our wills,
passing down our fortunes to the next generation. This card has
a strong connection with families and <u>inheritance.</u>

What does this card mean to you? When did you feel like you
had succeeded or made it in life?

The Celtic Cross Spread

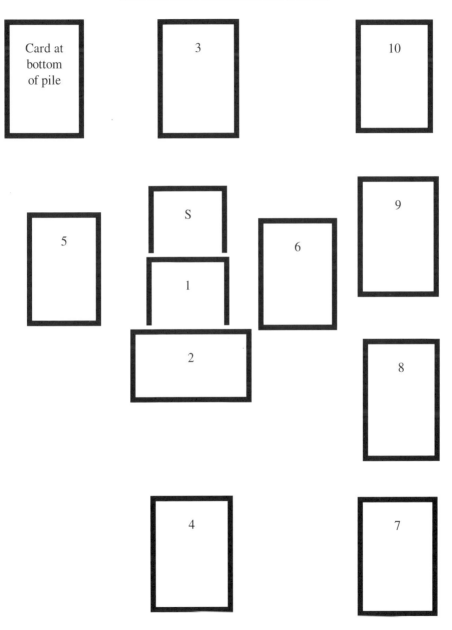

The Celtic Cross Spread

S. Significator - represents client according to star sign

1. Present situation
2. What blocks the situation
      Or
   Their Goal
3. Pressing Issues
4. Hidden Issues
5. Recent past
6. Immediate future
7. Answer to your question
8. Message from your guides
9. Hopes and fears
10. Final outcome

The Celtic cross is the best spread to use, when you want to give a general reading, covering all aspects of the clients life. It covers past, present and future and you can pick up a lot of different things happening in their life.

First of all, you need to find the king or queen that resembles your client, according to their star sign and place it in the centre of the spread.

Give the remaining cards to your client and ask them to shuffle, thinking of what is going on in their life at the moment and what they want to come up in the reading.

Whilst they are shuffling, you need to focus on their significator card. How does that card look to you today? What jumps out? Does the king or queen look happy, sad, worried.... Focus on any thoughts that come into your head, as random as they may be, remember it is your guides working with you. If you want to talk about children, work etc then do so - in time you will learn to trust your intuition and let it take over.

When your client has finished shuffling, ask him/her to put the deck down on the table and think of a question that he/she wants answering in her head. When he/she is ready, ask him/her to cut the pile into three separate piles on the table.

Ask him/her to choose a pile for you to work with, take that pile in your hand and move the other two piles out of the way (put them in one pile to the side, you may need them later).

Take the card at the bottom of the pile and put it at the top left hand side of the spread. This card tells you what the reading is going to be about. Talk to your client about the meaning of the card and what you feel it is saying to you.

Now lay out the Celtic cross spread as shown with all the cards facing down, so you cannot see the pictures. This is important because we don't want to worry the client with any of the cards towards the end of the reading without having had chance to explain why they are there. We don't want them to jump to conclusions.

Turn over 1 and 2 at the same time. These cards tell us of the current situation, or the most important thing spirit wants to talk about.

Card number 1 is where they are now, or what they are hoping to achieve. Card number 2 tells us what is blocking them from achieving their goal, or what the outcome is , depending on whether it is a good or bad card.

I always like to pull out one extra card from the unused pile to give me more in-depth information. Do this as soon as you have turned over the first two, to be able to give a full story.

Card number 3 is telling you what is in the front of their mind - the most important thing they are worrying about, or thinking about. It could well be completely different from the two first cards.

As with all of the cards, I like to use two or three other cards from the pile to give me more information. They end up telling me a more detailed story.

Card number 4 is telling you what is in the back of their mind - something they probably wouldn't expect to come up in the reading. A problem that they don't feel is that important to them, but it is still necessary to talk about. This also shows your credibility as a reader, as they most likely did not think of this whilst shuffling.

Card number 5 is their past. Study it carefully, as sometimes it is their immediate past, but sometimes, it goes back years, enabling you to understand the reason they approach life in the way they do. A sad insecure childhood, for example, a controlling father, leaving them fearful of men in adulthood and unsuccessful in relationships.

Card number 6 is the immediate future. This is telling them what is about to happen. They will only believe you here, if you have been accurate with the present and past!

Card number 7 is the answer to their question, so before you turn it over, ask them what the question was they thought of after shuffling the deck.

Card number 8 is probably the most important card in the entire reading for me. This is the message from their guides. Re ground yourself and listen very carefully to your inner voice as this one is important. This is advice you are passing on from spirit. I only tend to pull one extra card for this one.

Card number 9 represents their hopes and fears, good or bad. Again, these cards could pick up on another subject that you haven't yet covered. Study the cards carefully and notice what jumps out to make sure you are accurate.

The final card number 10 is the outcome to the general meaning of the reading. Pull a maximum of three cards out on this one to be able to give a full and detailed ending to the reading.

Finish by asking if the client has any more questions they want you to answer. If they say yes, pick up all the cards, including the pile that you didn't use and reshuffle the entire deck, whilst thinking of their question.

When you are ready, take the top three cards off the top of the pile for your answer.

Do this as many times as you need to make sure your client leaves, having covered all the areas in their life that they were concerned about.

Looking for Love Spread

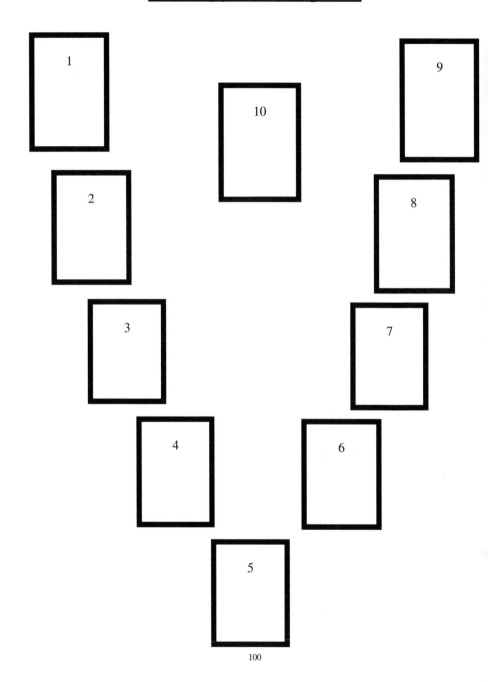

Looking For Love

1. What they have experienced in the past

2. What they need to learn from this

3. What they are experiencing now

4. What they are hoping for

5. What they actually need

6. What holds them back from achieving this

7. Their view of themselves

8. What they still need to learn

9. What they will experience next

10. The final outcome

Relationship Spread

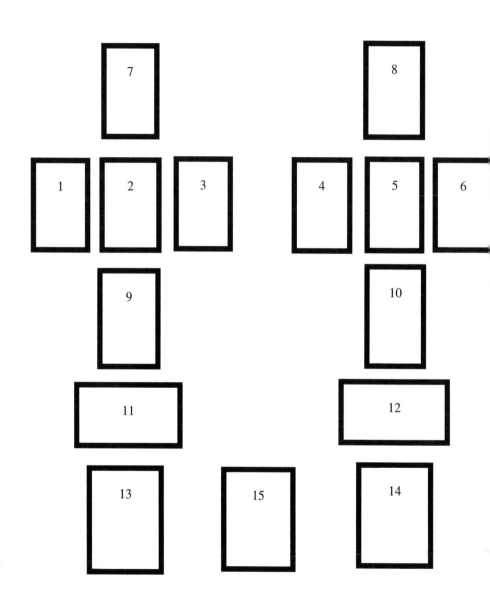

Relationship Spread

1. What she is bringing to the relationship

2. Where she stands now

3. What she is hoping to achieve in this relationship

4. What he is bringing to the relationship

5. Where he stands now

6. What he is hoping to achieve in this relationship

7. How she sees him

8. How he sees her

9. How she first saw him

10. How he first saw her

11. Her fears

12. His fears

13. Outside influences on her

14. Outside influences on him

15. Final Outcome

Being a modern professional tarot reader

Gone are the days when tarot was frightening, scary and misunderstood. The daunting pictures, and the fear of being told things that you don't want to hear, the thought that the tarot reader would curse you if she didn't take to you.

It is up to us to give a new face to tarot, to show people that tarot is a modern way of counselling.

First of all, make sure you are dressed casually and smartly. You need to come across as approachable and understanding and above all, normal!

Always work in love and light - the first thing you do is light a candle and cleanse your deck of cards each and every time you use them.
This removes the energy from the previous reading you did and keeps your cards cleansed.
Always keep your cards covered in cloth or in a box, out of sight to make sure nobody touches them.

Lighting a candle ensures you are working in the love and light, keeping both you and your client safe from negative energies .Remember these cards are a tool for spirit to communicate with you. When you get really good, you don't need to turn the cards over to see the pictures as you will be working clairvoyantly or with your intuition - just as mediums do.

Always see situations from the _positive_ angle. Even in the worst situation we have been through in life, we can look back and see good things that have come from that time. When you come across a hard time in someone's reading, always think back to a time in your own life where you struggled and remember how you felt yourself. Be sympathetic but positive , concentrate on finding a good solution instead of focusing on the upsetting situation itself.

Never read for a child, unless you have the permission of the parent. Even then I would not recommend it as children are too easily influenced.

Advise, but never tell anyone what to do. It is their life, their choices and decisions, we are only able to suggest solutions. There is no professional conduct given for tarot readers to follow like counsellors and financial advisers have, so we have to make our own highest standards and stick to them.

Never condemn anyone for an action or show your disapproval, such as a termination, an affair etc. You are in no position to judge or to look down on people, they have trusted you and come to you for answers. Try and feel what it is like to be in their shoes and give advice that you are channelling from spirit (intuition) not your own beliefs.

Finally, remember each reading you do is completely confidential.

Making the cards work together.

When you have got used to all of the cards and their meanings, then it is time to begin mixing them together in a reading. Cards work together and tell us a story about the life of the person we are reading for.

The first card you pull out tells you what area of their life we are talking about and the ones directly next to it tell us more details about that situation. So if we had a Cups card first then a Wands card next to it, we know that we are talking about a relationship but the wand card tells us what the problem or celebration is.

Ace of Cups

5 of Wands

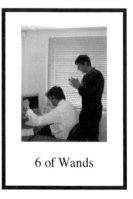

6 of Wands

The Ace of cups tells us we are talking about a romance or relationship, the five of wands is directly next to it, so this says there is conflict or a problem. However, the six of wands is there, so we know it will be a successful outcome and a happy ending. Thanks to this last card being there, we can now reassure them that everything will be okay.

Ace of Cups

5 of Wands

8 of Cups

Look how different the same story would be if the last card was the 8 of cups instead. Now the advice would be to give up and walk away, it isn't going to work.

10 of Cups

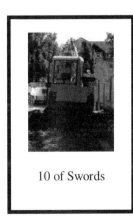

10 of Swords

6 - Lovers

If we had the 10 of cups first and the 10 of swords next to it, it would be telling us that a marriage has ended. The Lovers card tells me that one of them had an affair, that caused the marriage breakdown.

6 - Lovers

10 of Swords

10 of Cups

Look how different a story we have now. The same cards but in a different order now tell me that an affair has come to an unhappy end, however the 10 of cups tells me that the marriage will survive and they will get over it.

It takes time and practise to read more than one card together. Using more than one card is what makes us more detailed with our predictions. Instead of just announcing a happy event is coming up, we are able to tell them exactly what it is.

I like to use two or three extra cards on each one in a Celtic cross to be more detailed with my reading. You will find your own way eventually, always remember to take them from the top of the pile you have left over.

Keep practising by randomly picking two or three cards from your deck and by using the meaning for the first card, make up stories. This is the easiest and fastest way of learning the meanings to your cards.

The People Cards

Every star sign has different personalities and traits, some positive, some negative. Nobody is perfect! Getting to know how each king and queen think and look on life is important.

Water signs - the cups family, are gentle, sensitive, emotional people. They care deeply for their loved ones and manage to feel other people's pain. They find it difficult to let go of painful memories, always remembering how it felt to break up or fall out with someone. They need constant love and attention and often reassurance that they are loved back in a relationship.

Fire signs - the wands family, are passionate, dynamic, busy people always on a mission to succeed. They are hard workers never afraid of a long days work. They are risk takers to a certain degree, gambling to achieve their dreams. They can also get deeply heart but vow never to let the same situation happen again. They work to be successful for the recognition but would often give their last penny away as they don't do it for the money, just the feeling of success.

Air signs - the swords family, are the business people, clever strong and intellectual. They analyse every situation before they make a decision, which makes them clever people. They are devoted to their work, often making it to the top of their chosen profession, working well managing other people. They treat people and situations in a fair and just manner. These people have high morals and expect to be treated the way they treat others.

Earth signs - the pentacles family, are also good business people, being fantastic at making money. They are hard workers like the fire signs but they do it to be financially successful.

They love the good things in life and never expect hand outs - they know that if they want something, they have to work hard for it. They are creative, ambitious and have traditional values and standards.

We have to be able to laugh at our ways and understand that people aren't being difficult or obnoxious, they just have different ways of thinking. If you remember that we are all here to learn emotional lessons in life, maybe to right a wrong in a past life, or to learn a new emotion in this life, it seems to help in understanding why some star signs put all their energy into love and others aren't interested in that in the slightest, but just want to succeed in work and ambition! We have to learn to live along side each other in harmony, taking into consideration that we are all different and on a separate path in life, even when joined by marriage or family ties.

So on that note, you have to understand that the pages (children from 0 - 18) have come down with their own lessons to learn. Their personalities and ambitions have already been decided by their star sign, probably very different from yours.
Your job as a parent is to nurture them **not** change them into how you think children should be.
If you have a naughty child, you have to look at the guidance they have been given and see how that could change to be more understanding to the child. If you have a quiet shy child, this has to be understood as part of their personality, you cannot try and make this child into a public speaker!

Look at each page and make notes of which child you know or have known that come under that category. When a child does not fit the description, is there something wrong in that child's life? For example how would a happy go lucky page of wands react to upset in the family such as divorce? They need the truth given to them when asking questions as to why daddy doesn't live with them anymore. What would that child be like if the mother lied to try and make it easier without realising that their child isn't stupid and knows she is lying? Probably very angry, naughty and resentful at being lied to. Page of wands are very mature children, desperate to grow up - it is as if they have been round many times. Explaining the truth about divorce to one of these children wouldn't be as bad as you think, they would cope and adapt very quickly.

In the same situation, how would a page of pentacles cope? These gentle loving children would need constant cuddles, love and reassurance. Probably not as able to cope with losing someone as a page of wands. It would affect how they turn out as an adult and look at marriage, so plenty of attention is needed to ensure they marry happily one day themselves.

The knights in the four suits are the young adults, aged between 18 - 30. Their personalities are so different yet again and you have to remember that their childhood has moulded them into the person they are today. Think back to how you were at this age and what was important to you. To a knight of wands it is all about having fun, travelling and searching for answers. They are entertaining, great fun to be with, yet have a serious side to them that they don't often show. They all have great dreams of being successful and work hard.

A knight of cups is on the search for the perfect love, and takes each heartbreak very seriously and learns from it. They will still be able to talk about the pain of breaking up with a childhood sweetheart when they are in their forties. They are emotional people and see marriage completely differently to other star signs.

The queens in the tarot are so different from each other. The queen of cups is the maternal woman in the deck, the queen of wands is the busiest mother, needing to occupy her mind through work or social commitments at the same time as raising a family. The queen of swords is the business woman, with a fair and just outlook on life, raising children with the same attitude she uses for work - tolerant, sharp, clever and in control. The queen of pentacles is devoted to everything she does, always putting her children's needs first, whilst working to provide them with a good material life.

Don't forget that childhood has a huge impact on how you raise your own children. If you had an unhappy upbringing yourself, you would more than likely do everything in your power to not repeat history. However, what happens if some people know no different and continue to make mistakes like their parents did to them?

The kings in the deck are dynamic and masculine. They are so different from each other, with the king of cups being the sensitive, gentle water sign, the king of wands being the provider and the king of swords often being the professional strong suited and booted man. The king of pentacles is the family man, aiming to provide the best of the best for his family.

The kings and queens can also come out in a reading to represent us at different stages in our lives. For example, I am a queen of wands, yet the queen of cups often appears in my reading, to tell me I need to take time out to be more like her. i.e. a mother - it says spend quality time with your children as they need you.

If a queen of cups had the queen of wands come up in her reading, it might indicate a time when she was going to be more like her - taking on a job, making her a working woman, juggling career and children.

Try matching the kings and queens together and see what kind of a marriage they would have. Note the positive and the

negative points. A king of wands with a queen of cups would go together well, making a traditional family with a mother at home and the dad at work being the provider. However, the queen of cups is emotional and the king of wands is not, so the wife would often want more time with her busy working husband. She puts family first and he puts work first.
A king of pentacles with a queen of wands would be an interesting mix. The king wants to see his family brought up traditionally, yet the queen of wands is a busy dynamic lady, often working full time and loving every minute of her career. They both strive to provide the best for their family, yet there might be a bit of competition as to who's career is the most important.

So how would a queen of cups cope with a page of swords as her child, compared to a queen of wands? I think a queen of cups is sometimes too soft and gentle, as a boisterous child needs discipline and boundaries. However, a queen of wands is firmer and sets rules for her children. This doesn't make her a better mother though, as the love and tenderness a queen of cups gives is also essential for a page of swords.

Playing with the people cards and laying them out in families, helps you learn the pros and cons of different parents for each young child. Set out what your family was, with your parents and any brothers and sisters you have and see if it helps you understand your childhood a little better. There must be good points and bad points that you remember of your parents raising you. See if understanding their star signs, helps you see their point of view a little better, or realising why they were the way they were towards you as a child.

NOTES

NOTES

NOTES

NOTES

NOTES

NOTES